IS JESUS THE ONLY WAY?

IS JESUS THE ONLY WAY?

Philip Graham Ryken

CROSSWAY

WHEATON, ILLINOIS

Is Jesus the Only Way?

Copyright © 2012 by the Alliance of Confessing Evangelicals

Published by Crossway
    1300 Crescent Street
    Wheaton, Illinois 60187

The Alliance of Confessing Evangelicals exists to call the church, amidst our dying culture, to repent of its worldliness, to recover and confess the truth of God's Word as did the Reformers, and to see that truth embodied in doctrine, worship, and life.

Cover design: Dual Identity inc.

Cover image(s): iStock, Getty, Shutterstock

First printing 1999

Reprinted with new cover 2012

Printed in the United States of America

Scripture quotations are from The Holy Bible, New International Version®, NIV®. Copyright © 1973, 1978, 1984, by Biblica, Inc.™ Used by permission. All rights reserved worldwide.

Trade paperback ISBN: 978-1-4335-2975-7
PDF ISBN: 978-1-4335-2976-4
Mobipocket ISBN: 978-1-4335-2977-1
ePub ISBN: 978-1-4335-2978-8

Library of Congress Cataloging-in-Publication Data
Ryken, Philip Graham, 1966–
 Is Jesus the only way? / Philip Graham Ryken.
 p. cm. — (Today's issues)
 Includes bibliographical references.
 ISBN 1-58134-119-9 (booklet)
 1. Evangelicalism. 2. Religious pluralism—Christianity.
I. Title. II. Series: Today's Issues (Wheaton, IL)
BR1640.R95 2000
261.2—dc21   99-36909

Crossway is a publishing ministry of Good News Publishers.

VP		20	19	18	17	16	15	14	13	12
14	13	12	11	10	9	8	7	6	5	4	3	2	1

CONTENTS

Preface   7

1   The Problem with Christians   11

2   Three Kinds of Pluralism   15

3   When Pluralism Comes to Church   25

4   Christianity for a Pluralistic Age   29

5   Why Jesus Is the Only Way   39

For Further Reading   59

PREFACE

These are not good days for the evangelical church, and anyone who steps back from what is going on for a moment to try to evaluate our life and times will understand that.

In the last few years a number of important books have been published all trying to understand what is happening, and they are saying much the same thing even though the authors come from fairly different backgrounds and are doing different work. One is by David F. Wells, a theology professor at Gordon-Conwell Theological Seminary in Massachusetts. It is called *No Place for Truth*. A second is by Michael Scott Horton, vice president of the Alliance of Confessing Evangelicals. His book is called *Power Religion*. The third is by the well-known pastor of Grace Community Church in California, John F. MacArthur. It is called *Ashamed of the Gospel*. Each of these authors is writing about the evangelical church, not the liberal church, and a person can get an idea of what each is saying from the titles alone.

Yet the subtitles are even more revealing. The subtitle

of Wells's book reads *Or Whatever Happened to Evangelical Theology?* The subtitle of Horton's book is *The Selling Out of the Evangelical Church*. The subtitle of John MacArthur's work proclaims, *When the Church Becomes Like the World*.

When you put these together, you realize that these careful observers of the current church scene perceive that today evangelicalism is seriously off base because it has abandoned its evangelical truth-heritage. The thesis of David Wells's book is that the evangelical church is either dead or dying as a significant religious force because it has forgotten what it stands for. Instead of trying to do God's work in God's way, it is trying to build a prosperous earthly kingdom with secular tools. Thus, in spite of our apparent success we have been "living in a fool's paradise," Wells declared in an address to the National Association of Evangelicals in 1995.

John H. Armstrong, a founding member of the Alliance of Confessing Evangelicals, has edited a volume titled *The Coming Evangelical Crisis*. When he was asked not long afterwards whether he thought the crisis was still coming or is actually here, he admitted that in his judgment the crisis is already upon us.

The Alliance of Confessing Evangelicals is addressing this problem through seminars and conferences, radio programs, *modern* REFORMATION magazine, Reformation Societies, and scholarly writings. The series of booklets on today's issues is a further effort along these same lines. If you are troubled by the state of today's church and are helped by these booklets, we invite you to contact the Alliance at 1716 Spruce Street, Philadelphia, PA 19103. You can also phone us at 215-546-3696 or visit the Alliance at our website: www. AllianceNet.org. We would like to work with you under God "for a modern Reformation."

James Montgomery Boice
Alliance of Confessing Evangelicals

CHAPTER ONE

THE PROBLEM WITH CHRISTIANS

The problem with Christians is that they insist they have the only way to salvation. Sometimes they talk about being "born again." Sometimes they tell you to "believe in Jesus." But it all boils down to the same thing in the end: Christians think they worship the only true God.

But how can Jesus be the *only* way? Is Christianity anything more than narrow-minded bigotry?

One writer who objects to the uniqueness of Christianity is Alan Watts. Once a minister in the Anglican church, Watts gradually grew disaffected with the Christian church and was attracted to Eastern religions such as Buddhism and Hinduism. He has now written some twenty books trying to combine the religions of the world into one universal faith.

Over time Watts has found Christianity strangely resistant to being incorporated into a global religion. In the end he has had to leave it behind altogether. As he writes in the preface to *Beyond Theology*:

> There is not a scrap of evidence that the Christian hierarchy was ever aware of itself as one among several lines of transmission for a universal tradition. Christians . . . did not take at all kindly to ideas that even begin to question the unique and supreme position of the historical Jesus. . . . Christianity is a contentious faith which requires an all-or-nothing commitment to Jesus as the one and only incarnation of the Son of God. . . . My previous discussions did not take proper account of that whole aspect of Christianity which is uncompromising, ornery, militant, rigorous, imperious and invincibly self-righteous. They did not give sufficient weight to the church's disagreeable insistence on the reality of a totally malignant spirit of cosmic evil, on everlasting damnation and on the absolute distinction between Creator and creature. These thorny and objectionable facets of Christianity cannot be shrugged off as temporary distortions or errors. (New York: World Publishing, 1967, p. xii)

Watts is right about one thing at least. Christianity is the one piece of luggage that refuses to be stuffed into his theological trunk. It requires an all-or-nothing commitment to Jesus Christ.

Authentic, biblical Christianity has always been an exclusive religion. This became apparent during the Roman Empire. When the Emperor Alexander Severus heard about Christianity, he placed an image of Christ beside the other gods in his private chapel, just to be safe. The Romans were happy to welcome Jesus into their pantheon.

What the Romans could not understand was why Christians refused to reciprocate. If the emperor was willing to worship Christ, why weren't Christians willing to worship the emperor? Yet the early Christians insisted that in order to worship Christ at all, they had to worship Christ *alone*. They were even willing to stand up for this conviction by playing "Christians and lions" at the Colosseum.

Jesus Christ refuses to have any colleagues. This is why Christianity has always seemed like such a scandalous religion. It is scandalous in the sense of the Greek word *skandal*, meaning "that which gives offense or arouses opposition." The crucifixion of Jesus Christ is "a stumbling block" to those outside the Christian faith (1 Cor. 1:23). For the past 2,000 years, Christianity's claims about the unique truth of Jesus Christ have aroused no end of opposition from Jews, pagans, Muslims, Communists, humanists, and atheists.

Insisting that Jesus is the only way is an especially unpopular stance in a culture based on freedom of choice. After all, our culture invented shopping malls and mail-order catalogs, where anything and everything is for sale. Religion is now called a "preference," which makes it sound like a soft drink or a shade of paint. If you can go to the college of your choice, root for the football team of your choice, watch the cable channel of your choice, and eat the yogurt of your choice, why can't you pray to the god of your choice?

These are fair questions. If Christians are going to insist that their religion is true—and that all other religions are false—then they have some explaining to do. The rest of this booklet was written to help explain how Jesus can be the only way.

CHAPTER TWO

THREE KINDS OF PLURALISM

One reason people are skeptical about the claims of Christ is that postmodern culture values religious pluralism. Donald A. Carson has tried to explain what this pluralism means for Christianity in a book called *The Gagging of God: Christianity Confronts Pluralism* (Grand Rapids, Mich.: Zondervan, 1996).

Empirical Pluralism

Carson begins by describing three different kinds of pluralism. The first he calls *empirical pluralism*, by which he means the fact that we live in a diverse society. America is a country of many languages, ethnicities, religions, and worldviews. As many as a dozen different languages are spoken in the hallways of many urban schools. Thus it is now more accurate to speak of American cultures than American culture.

We are living in increasingly post-Christian times. Christianity has lost its position as the dominant religious viewpoint in America. Partly this is because more Americans than ever before claim to be atheists or agnostics. At the same time, there is a New Age resurgence of paganism and the religions of the East. Islam is now among the fastest-growing religions in America. Still another reason for the decline of Christianity is the proliferation of cults such as Mormonism or the Jehovah's Witnesses.

Christianity is also losing its cultural force because so many people are making up their religion as they go along. In *Habits of the Heart* Robert Bellah reports on an interview with a young nurse who described her religion as "Sheilaism": "I believe in God. I'm not a religious fanatic. I can't remember the last time I went to church. My faith has carried me a long way. It's Sheilaism. Just my own little voice" (Berkeley, Calif.: University of California Press, 1985, pp. 232-233). In America there seem to be almost as many religions as there are citizens.

The radical privatization of religion means that America is more religiously diverse than ever. Thousands of different cults, sects, and fringe religions have their own computer websites. When religious diversity is added to ethnic and linguistic diversity, the result is empirical pluralism, one of the inescapable facts of our social existence.

Cherished Pluralism

A second kind of pluralism Carson terms *cherished pluralism*. Cherished pluralism goes beyond the empirical fact of pluralism to its value. To cherish pluralism is to appreciate it, welcome it, celebrate it, and approve of it. It says that pluralism exists, and it's a good thing too.

Pluralism is high on the postmodern agenda. University admissions departments try to make sure that each incoming class has diverse talents, interests, and backgrounds. Cities promote diversity by hosting parades, concerts, and exhibits, and by engaging in hiring practices that celebrate the divergent ethnic and cultural heritage of their citizens. Politicians appeal to multicultural diversity in their speeches and legislation. As a result of these efforts, pluralism is now among the most treasured of all values.

It is only a short step from cherishing cultural diversity to cherishing religious diversity. Perhaps the only reason religions differ is because cultures differ. In a speech at the 1993 Parliament of World Religions, Swami Chindanansa of the Divine Life Society argued that all religions are to be valued equally because they are all equally valuable. "There are many effective, equally valid religions," he said. "They are to be equally reverenced, equally recognized, and equally loved and cherished—not merely tolerated."

The view that all religions are equally valuable is becoming increasingly popular. Indeed, as the Christian missionary statesman Leslie Newbigin observes:

> It has become a commonplace to say that we live in a pluralist society—not merely a society which is in fact plural in the variety of cultures, religions and lifestyles which it embraces, but pluralist in the sense that this plurality is celebrated as a thing to be approved and cherished. (*The Gospel in a Pluralist Society*, Grand Rapids, Mich.: Eerdmans, 1989, p. 1)

One of the best examples of cherished religious pluralism comes from the mind of that great American theologian, Marilyn Monroe. Marilyn once was asked if she believed in God. With a flirtatious grin she said, "I just believe in everything—a little bit." This "Monroe doctrine" might be the defining doctrine of postmodern times.

Many Americans are eclectic in their moral and religious beliefs. They have a total disdain for logical consistency. They believe in being nice to animals, a woman's right to choose, their own basic goodness, the necessity of sexual gratification, being loyal to friends, and rooting for their favorite NBA team. They believe in everything a little bit, and especially in looking out for Number One. They even believe in the existence of God (or at least they say they do). But this hodge-podge of conviction is not organized into a coherent worldview. Nor can it be.

Philosophical Pluralism

A third kind of pluralism is *philosophical pluralism*. To review: empirical pluralism is a fact, and cherished pluralism values that fact. Philosophical pluralism goes one step further and demands it.

1. *The creed of pluralism.* Philosophical pluralism takes the fact of pluralism and turns it into a mind-set. It is the ideology that refuses to allow any single religion or worldview to claim an exclusive hold on the truth. It denies that there are any absolutes. It insists that all religions and worldviews must be seen as equally valid. According to Carson, philosophical pluralism holds that "any notion that a particular ideological or religious claim is intrinsically superior to another is necessarily wrong. The only absolute creed is the creed of pluralism. No religion has the right to pronounce itself right or true, and the others false" (p. 19). To put it another way, your worldview is just your opinion.

One theologian who has become famous—or perhaps infamous—for defending philosophical pluralism is John Hick. Hick believes that true religion is like a grand mosaic.

No single religion is capable of teaching us everything we need to know about God, but each religion gives us part of the picture. In his own words, "Each of the great world faiths constitutes a perception of and a response to the ultimate divine reality which they all in their different ways affirm" (*Christian Century*, vol. 98, p. 46).

In 1993 a shrine to philosophical pluralism was built on the campus of Vanderbilt University. The All Faith Chapel was dedicated by Hindus, Jews, Catholics, Protestants, Muslims, the Baha'i, and the Orthodox Christian Fellowship.

No religious symbolism is incorporated into the chapel's design. However, storage cabinets are provided to accommodate the accoutrements of various worship traditions. Thus each religious group can transform the chapel into its own worship space. Jewish students go to the cupboard and get out a menorah and a Torah scroll. Muslim students pull out a prayer mat and some copies of the Koran. Christians get out a cross and some Bibles. One might say that Vanderbilt students come out of the closet every time they worship!

Vanderbilt built the All Faith Chapel as a matter of principle. The board members of the university refused to build a chapel for only one religion. That would be narrow and sectarian. Instead, they insisted on supporting all religions at once. At the chapel's dedication, university chaplain Beverly Asbury said, "This place is for all faiths. Its dedication consists of many acts and of one. There is diversity in our unity, and there is unity in our diversity as we dedicate this space and add to its light, each in the way of a distinctive tradition." That is the creed of pluralism at its most self-contradictory: diversity in unity and unity in diversity.

2. *Is truth relative?* Another name for philosophical pluralism is relativism. It insists that all religious viewpoints are equally valid and equally true. To suggest otherwise is to be arrogant and intolerant. No religion can claim to be superior to any other. You may practice your faith as long as you realize it is only one of many true faiths. If what you believe is true at all, it is only relatively true.

Philosophical pluralism prefers to view the different religions of the world as different roads up the same mountain. They all lead to the mountaintop. Eventually Buddhists, Hindus, Muslims, and Christians will discover that they all worship the same God.

Or perhaps true religion is like the elephant in John Godfrey Saxe's poem "The Blind Men and the Elephant." The poem describes how six blind men of Indostan wanted to learn what an elephant was like. Each explored a different part of the animal, and each described it in a different way. When examined from the side the elephant seemed like a wall. From its tusk it seemed like a spear; from its trunk, like a snake; from its leg, a tree; from its ear, a fan; from its tail, a rope.

IS JESUS THE ONLY WAY?

And so these men of Indostan
Disputed loud and long,
Each in his own opinion
Exceeded stiff and strong
Though each was partly in the right
And all were in the wrong!

Saxe was using his poem to make a theological point. People who argue about religion are like blind men who "prate about an elephant not one of them has seen!"

One of the implications of pluralism as a philosophy is that it does not matter which religion you choose. Truth is relative. Since all worldviews are equally valid, you should choose whichever one is right for you. As President Eisenhower famously said, the American system of government makes no sense "unless it is founded in a deeply felt religious faith—and I don't care which one it is."

The philosophy of pluralism was portrayed in the film *Man Friday* (1975), based on Daniel DeFoe's explicitly Christian novel *Robinson Crusoe* (1719). In the film, the man Friday represents the ideal of religious pluralism. "Worship any way you like," he says, "as long as you mean it. God won't mind."

Really? How does the pluralist know what kind of worship God will accept? The suggestion that God doesn't care how he is worshiped is rather presumptuous. Indeed, this shows how smug pluralism can be. Although it claims to be humble about its ability to grasp religious truth, philosophical pluralism has an arrogance all its own. By declaring that doctrine is unimportant, it is condescending toward the truth-claims of every other religion.

At the same time that philosophical pluralism denies other religions the right to lay claim to the truth, it presents its own worldview as the absolute truth. Consider the story of the blind men and the elephant again. Dick Keyes of L'Abri Fellowship in Massachusetts offers a clever twist on this illustration. In one of his lectures he points out that whereas the men investigating the elephant are all blind, the pluralist has perfect vision. Like some sort of cosmic zookeeper he is able to see the whole elephant. He—and he alone—has the perception to know exactly what each religion contributes to the truth. In the end philosophical pluralism's dismissal of dogma turns out to be just another dogma.

CHAPTER THREE

WHEN PLURALISM COMES TO CHURCH

Christians have always been vulnerable to the latest ideas. Since the idea of pluralism has become so dominant in recent years, it comes as no surprise that it is beginning to influence the theology of the church.

Our pluralistic culture has rather naturally produced a pluralistic theology. Many people who call themselves Christians are now trying to find salvation outside the church as well as inside. They are looking for a way to embrace other religions without giving up their Christianity.

At least since Vatican II, religious pluralism has been the explicit goal of Roman Catholicism. The official teachings of the Roman Catholic Church still state there is no salvation except through Jesus Christ. However, the church also believes it is unnecessary for everyone to possess a conscious knowledge of Christ in order to experience redemption.

Pluralistic Christianity is also starting to attract a following among those who identify themselves as evangelicals. According to a study carried out by James Davison Hunter of the University of Virginia, a majority of students at Christian colleges and seminaries doubt whether faith in Jesus Christ is really necessary for salvation. Because of their concern for "those who have never heard," they hope that God will save all good people when they die, whether they have a personal relationship with Jesus Christ or not.

In the past, Christians expressed their concern for the heathen by throwing their efforts into missions and evangelism. Now some of them wonder if all that effort is really necessary. "How can God condemn those who have never heard the Gospel?" they wonder. "Maybe he saves them a different way. Maybe he gives them a chance after they die depending on how they lived their lives."

This speculative and rather sentimental view is defended in Clark Pinnock's book *A Wideness in God's Mercy: The Finality of Jesus Christ in a World of Religions* (Grand Rapids, Mich.: Zondervan, 1992). Pinnock identifies himself as an evangelical Christian. Yet he argues that Christianity is not the only valid religion. The other religions of the world offer true but partial salvation.

The argument goes something like this: The Bible says Jesus Christ is the Savior of the whole world (1 John 2:2). Yet not everyone in the world has the chance to hear the good news about Jesus Christ. Therefore Christ's saving presence must be revealed through other religions. Jesus can save people through Buddhism and Hinduism as well as through the Christian church. Pinnock thus rejects the exclusivity of Christ, arguing instead for what he calls the "finality of Christ." Christ will save (nearly) everyone in the end.

What, then, is the role of faith in Christ? Explicit faith in Jesus Christ is unnecessary. God's mercy is so wide that it embraces people of other faiths. All that is required is an "implicit faith" in Christ. In other words, many people would believe in Christ if they only had the opportunity. "The Bible does not teach that one must confess the name of Jesus to be saved," writes Pinnock. "One does not have to be conscious of the work of Christ done on one's behalf in order to benefit from that work. The issue God cares about is the direction of the heart, not the content of the theology" (p. 158).

Pinnock's brand of Christian pluralism is riddled with logical and theological errors, a few of which will be mentioned in the final chapter of this booklet. For the moment, however, it is enough to notice how odd this view is. Pluralistic Christianity argues that the religions of the world are full of anonymous Christians worshiping an unknown Christ. It thus asks us to agree that someone can be saved by Christ without knowing Christ, as if someone can believe in Christ without actually believing in him at all.

27

CHAPTER FOUR

CHRISTIANITY FOR A PLURALISTIC AGE

Enough has been said about the problem of pluralism, both inside and outside the church. It is time to start giving some answers. What does the Bible teach about pluralism? And how should Christians live in a pluralistic age?

The answer to these questions partly depends on what kind of pluralism is meant—the fact of empirical pluralism, the value of cherished pluralism, or the demand of philosophical pluralism. Reformation Christianity recognizes empirical pluralism and tolerates cherished pluralism but rejects any form of philosophical or religious pluralism.

The Same Old Story

In the first place, Christianity recognizes the fact of empirical pluralism. Christians recognize the ethnic, cultural, and religious diversity of modern culture. Pluralism is not some startling new discovery for Christianity. The diverse religions of the world do not pose a new challenge. On the contrary, Christians have always had to argue for the truth of Christianity over against other religions.

The Bible was written in a pluralistic context. Worshiping foreign gods was a constant temptation for God's people in Israel. Idolatry was extremely fashionable. Yet all through the Old Testament God insisted that his people turn away from idols to worship him alone.

The great general Joshua gave the people of Israel this choice:

> *If serving the LORD seems undesirable to you, then choose for yourselves this day whom you will serve, whether the gods your forefathers served beyond the River, or the gods of the Amorites, in whose land you are living. But as for me and my household, we will serve the LORD. (Josh. 24:15)*

Joshua's people did not make their choice out of ignorance; they were familiar with the religious options. To choose for God was to reject the alternatives.

The same was true in the days of the prophet Elijah. When he confronted the prophets of Baal on Mount Carmel, he gave the Israelites the same choice Joshua had given them: "How long will you waver between two opinions? If the LORD is God, follow him; but if Baal is God, follow him" (1 Kings 18:21). The people of God in the Old Testament needed constant reminders of God's uniqueness because they were surrounded by foreign gods and goddesses—Astarte, Chemosh, Molech, Rimmon, and a host of other deities.

The same was true throughout the New Testament. The global village is not a new address for Christianity. The first Christians lived in cosmopolitan cities like Antioch, Corinth, and Rome, at the crossroads of multicultural exchange in the ancient world. This means they were surrounded by other worldviews. They were not Christians because they had never heard of anything else. Rather, they were converts to Christianity *from* other religions. When they said, "Jesus is the only way," they knew what the other ways were. They were always explaining and defending Christianity over against Judaism, eastern mystery religions, Roman imperial cults, and the various schools of Greek philosophy.

A good example of the clash between Christianity and other worldviews comes from the book of Acts. Chapter 17 tells the story of what happened when the missionary Paul visited Athens, the intellectual center of the Mediterranean world. As the historian who wrote the book of Acts wryly observed, "All the Athenians and the foreigners who lived there spent their time doing nothing but talking about and listening to the latest ideas" (v. 21).

Not surprisingly, Paul quickly entered into a dispute with some Epicurean and Stoic philosophers. Since philosophers like nothing better than a good argument, they invited Paul to a meeting of the Areopagus, the famous philosophical society that met on Mars Hill, overlooking the city.

Paul had seen many pagan altars in the Athenian marketplace. So he began his seminar by acknowledging how religious the Greeks were:

> *"Men of Athens! I see that in every way you are very religious. For as I walked around and observed your objects of worship, I even found an altar with this inscription: TO AN UNKNOWN GOD." (vv. 22-23)*

Paul proceeded to explain Christianity to the philosophers of the Areopagus. But he did not say, "Here, let me tell you about another god to add to your pantheon." Instead, he insisted that his God made all other gods obsolete. "The God who made the world and everything in it is the Lord of heaven and earth and does not live in temples built by hands. And he is not served by human hands, as if he needed anything, because he himself gives all men life and breath and everything else" (vv. 24-25). Since he is the one who gives life and breath to everyone, the true and living God supersedes all other gods.

Paul's point is that religious pluralism is ruled out by

Christianity. Making representations of the supreme divine being in gold or silver or stone is an act of sheer ignorance. And not only is such promiscuous worship ignorant, it is morally culpable. "We should not think that the divine being is like gold or silver or stone—an image made by man's design and skill. In the past God overlooked such ignorance, but now he commands all people everywhere to repent" (vv. 29-30). Nor should we think that only ignorant savages worship dumb idols. In our supposed sophistication we worship lesser things like affluence and personal space. The twenty-first century seems poised for a new outbreak of true paganism.

Paul was well aware of the main ideas of pagan philosophy and religion. He was honest about the challenge of pluralism, and thus he was able to meet it head-on. Throughout his defense he presented Christianity over against the background of empirical pluralism, as Christians must do to this very day.

Tolerance Is a Virtue

When it comes to cherished pluralism, Christians are often willing to cherish it themselves. They certainly cherish cultural diversity.

1. *Cultural diversity.* At the Tenth Presbyterian Church in Philadelphia, new members are welcomed to the congregation every quarter. As many as twenty-five or thirty new members will line up at the front of the church to give a

public testimony of their faith in Jesus Christ. Normally the new members come from the African-American, Caucasian, and Hispanic communities of Phila-delphia. Sometimes they also include African, Asian, or Indian converts. As they stand at the front of the church, these new members are a visible reminder that the family of God is ethnically and culturally diverse. As Christians we not only permit such diversity, but we *cherish* it. This is because God himself cherishes ethnic diversity. He is not *color-blind;* he is *colorful.* At his throne God welcomes worshipers "from every nation, tribe, people and language" (Rev. 7:9). His plan of redemption is for the peoples of the world in all their rich variety. He is establishing a new humanity in which "there is neither Jew nor Greek, slave nor free, male nor female, for you are all one in Christ Jesus" (Gal. 3:28).

It is worth noting that Christianity is already the most universal of all religions. There is nothing ethnocentric about authentic Christianity. It would be a serious mistake to view it as a Western religion. Christianity not only comes from the Middle East, but its center of gravity has shifted away from Europe and North America to Africa, Asia, and Latin America. Christianity is a truly global religion, in part because Christians cherish the diversity they have as spiritual brothers and sisters.

2. *Religious diversity.* So much for cultural diversity. What

about religious pluralism? To cherish *that* would mean the death of Christianity. A Christianity that loses its hold on the exclusive claims of Christ ceases to be Christianity at all.

However, although Christians cannot cherish religious pluralism, they must tolerate it. Since this is often misunderstood—both inside and outside the church—it is worth emphasizing: Christianity insists on religious tolerance.

By tolerance I mean allowing other people to hold and to defend their own religious convictions. Tolerance does not mean that everyone has to agree with everyone else. That would not be tolerance at all. The word *tolerance* itself assumes disagreement, that there is something that must be tolerated.

Tolerance thus applies to persons, but not to their errors. It does not require me to endorse your worldview. If you are not a Christian, I do not endorse your worldview. In the context of a friendship I will even try to talk you out of it.

But Christianity is not a coercive or manipulative religion. "Rather, we have renounced secret and shameful ways; we do not use deception, nor do we distort the word of God. On the contrary, by setting forth the truth plainly we commend ourselves to every man's conscience in the sight of God" (2 Cor. 4:2-3). True Christianity advances by persuasion rather than by force. It teaches that every human being must decide for or against God. It recognizes that faith in God requires a change of heart that only comes through the gift of God's Spirit (Eph.

2:8-9). Thus it respects human freedom, including the freedom of the non-Christian.

Religious tolerance is written into the First Amendment to the Constitution of the United States. This is good theology as well as good governance. It is legitimate for the government to legislate moral conduct. But it is not legitimate—indeed, it is impossible—for the government to enforce private belief. Pluralism, rightly understood, respects other people's convictions. It recognizes that there are important religious issues to be discussed and even argued about. Yet it carries out these arguments with humility and civility.

3. *Tolerance and truth.* Unfortunately, some Christians are intolerant, as everyone knows. The English essayist Jonathan Swift once bitterly observed, "We have just enough religion to make us hate, but not enough to make us love one another."

There are many examples of Christian intolerance from history—the Crusades, the religious wars of Europe, anti-Semitism, and so forth. Though they are often persecuted themselves, Christians have done more than their share of the persecuting. The Swiss Roman Catholic theologian Hans Küng is right to say that "blind zeal for truth in all periods and in all churches and religions has ruthlessly injured, burned, destroyed and murdered" (*Journal of Theology for Southern Africa*, vol. 56, p. 4).

Intolerant Christianity cannot be defended. It is not genuine Christianity at all. Intolerant Christians are either bad Christians or simply not Christians at all. Jesus said, "Do not resist an evil person. If someone strikes you on the right cheek, turn to him the other also. . . . Love your enemies and pray for those who persecute you, that you may be sons of your Father in heaven" (Matt. 5:39, 44-45). If that is the kind of love Christians should have for violent enemies, they should have even more love for people who simply hold a different philosophy of life. Tolerance is a virtue, especially for Christians.

True Christianity thus preserves a powerful combination that is found nowhere else: tolerance *and* truth.

Some religions and most political philosophies claim to have the truth but are ruthlessly intolerant of those who disagree. They offer truth without tolerance.

Philosophical pluralism, on the other hand, is indifferent to the truth. It provides a pound of tolerance without an ounce of truth. It is perfectly happy to allow people to believe whatever they want, even things that are mutually contradictory, as long as no one steps on anyone else's worldview. Philosophical pluralism idolizes tolerance while it eliminates the truth, although curiously it also tends to be intolerant of people—for example, Christians—who have strong religious convictions.

Ultimately Christians reject the demand of philosophical pluralism because they prize both tolerance and truth.

Philosophical pluralism is where worldviews collide. When Christianity is treated as only one among many equally true and valid religions, Christians start to become, as Alan Watts put it, "uncompromising, ornery, militant [and] rigorous" in their defense of the truth.

CHAPTER FIVE

WHY JESUS IS THE ONLY WAY

The reason philosophical pluralism makes Christians ornery is that it would force them to abandon truth. There are at least four essential beliefs that Christianity refuses to leave behind: the unity of truth, the uniqueness of Jesus Christ, the reality of sin, and the absolute necessity of the atonement.

The Only Truth

Christianity rejects philosophical pluralism because it accepts the Truth, with a capital T. There is only one truth, and that truth is one. As the apostle Paul explained, "We cannot do anything against the truth, but only for the truth" (2 Cor. 13:8).

IS JESUS THE ONLY WAY?

The Archbishop of Canterbury and the actress Jane Fonda once had an exchange that illustrates how Christians understand truth:

> The Archbishop of Canterbury: "Jesus is the Son of God, you know."
> Jane Fonda: "Maybe he is for you, but he's not for me."
> The Archbishop of Canterbury: "Well, either he is or he isn't."

Jane Fonda evidently believes in philosophical pluralism. Perhaps her view should be termed "Fonda-mentalism." What is true for you may not be true for her, and vice versa.

As a Christian, the Archbishop of Canterbury rightly insisted that truth cannot contradict itself. Either Jesus is the Son of God and the Savior of the world, or he is not. It is one or the other; it cannot be both.

To believe that two contradictory religions are both true is like saying, "2 + 2 = 4, or 5, or 37, or whatever you like." To believe all religions simultaneously is to become hopelessly entangled in self-contradiction. One simply cannot accept the Hindu belief that there are 300,000 or more gods and at the same time accept the Muslim belief that there is only one god. Nor can one embrace either Hinduism or Islam *and* Buddhism because historic Buddhism does not believe in a personal God at all.

Or consider religious opinions about the afterlife. Buddhists seek Nirvana, the complete absence of desire. Christianity teaches that heaven is a place where all pure desires are satisfied in Jesus Christ (Rev. 22:4). Who is right? If there is a heaven at all, does it negate or satisfy desire?

Opinions about judgment differ as well. Christianity teaches that "man is destined to die once, and after that to face judgment" (Heb. 9:27). Hindus believe in a seemingly endless series of reincarnations. Well, which is it? Both views cannot be true.

Religion is not a preference. Although people are allowed to hold their own opinions, they cannot make up their own truth. This cannot be done with religion any more than it can be done with mathematics. To insist that all religions are equally true is another way of saying that all religions are equally false. Somewhere in his *Religion and Society Report*, Harold O. J. Brown has observed that pluralism "purports to respect all ideas and opinions, but in the last analysis ends by denying that any idea or any conviction has validity." If every religion is compatible with its opposite, why bother with religion at all?

One is reminded of Edward Gibbon's comment that in the last days of the Roman Empire, "all religions were regarded by the people as equally true, by the philosophers as equally false, and by the politicians as equally useful." Gibbon's remark is an apt summary of pluralism in these postmodern times. It is also an accurate historical generalization about religion in Rome, though it cannot be applied to Roman Christians of that era. They at least maintained that there is only one Truth.

The Only Savior

A second belief Christians refuse to abandon is that Jesus is the only Savior. The reason Christians make this claim is because Jesus himself made it. In John's biography of Jesus— his Gospel as it is called—Jesus says, "I am the gate; whoever enters through me will be saved" (10:9). On another occasion he said, "I am the way and the truth and the life. No one comes to the Father except through me" (John 14:6). These statements were made to skeptics, to people who wondered which religion was true. Jesus was presenting himself as the skeptic's answer.

1. *Christianity is exclusive.* The statements Jesus made are exclusive. He claimed to be the gate, the way, the truth, the life. He was insisting that one must go through him to be saved. There is no other gate, way, truth, life, or salvation.

By making these statements Jesus was identifying himself with the Lord God of the Hebrew Scriptures. In the Old Testament God said, "Turn to me and be saved, all you ends of the earth; for I am God, and there is no other" (Isa. 45:22). There is only one God and one Savior of the world. In the New

Testament, Jesus Christ claims to be that unique Savior; he claims to be God.

The uniqueness of Jesus Christ is emphasized in another famous quotation from John's Gospel, John 3:16. Incidentally, if you are not a Christian this may help answer one of life's great questions. Frequently when there is a major sporting event on television someone holds up a sign that reads "John 3:16." Here is why: In that verse Jesus says, "For God so loved the world that he gave his one and only Son, that whoever believes in him shall not perish but have eternal life."

That is as good a short summary of Christianity as there is. Christianity teaches that out of his great love God sent his only Son, Jesus Christ, into the world. Everyone who accepts God's Son will live forever with God. If you believe in him, you get to go to heaven. Otherwise you will perish. Quite simply, faith in Jesus Christ is a matter of life or death. As the Bible goes on to say, "Whoever believes in him is not condemned, but whoever does not believe stands condemned already because he has not believed in the name of God's one and only Son" (v. 18; cf. 8:24).

"God so loved the world that he gave his . . . only Son." This is Christianity at both its narrowest and its broadest. On the one hand, Christianity is the most exclusive religion imaginable. It insists that belief in Jesus Christ is absolutely necessary for salvation. Jesus is the *only* way. You must go to him to get eternal life.

2. *Christianity is inclusive.* On the other hand, Christianity is the most inclusive religion possible because it makes salvation accessible to everyone. Salvation is offered for all people through one person. Whoever believes in him will not perish. Anyone who receives or believes in Jesus will live forever with God. There are no racial, social, intellectual, or economic criteria that prevent anyone from joining God's family.

One of the problems with the other religions of the world is that they all smack of elitism. Hinduism has its caste system. Judaism requires keeping the Torah. Islam requires following the Five Pillars of Obedience. Buddhism requires reaching a level of enlightenment. But what if you don't qualify? What if you are poor, immoral, disobedient, or unenlightened? What then? Only Christianity offers salvation to *everyone* as a free gift.

There is nothing elitist about Christianity. It is inclusive and exclusive at the same time. The particularity of Christ should not hide his universality. Although he is the only way to God, he offers the Gospel to everyone. "There is one God and one mediator between God and men, the man Christ Jesus, who gave himself as a ransom for all men" (1 Tim. 2:5-6). Whoever you are, you may and you must come close to God through Jesus Christ.

To use an analogy, Jesus is like God's telephone number. The God of the universe can only be contacted through Jesus

Christ. Philosophical pluralists insist on getting through to God no matter what number they dial. But that is not how the telephone system operates, and it is not how God operates either. Jesus is the only direct line to God.

This is where faith comes in. To know God is to trust in Jesus Christ. Earlier we mentioned the view that explicit faith in Jesus Christ is unnecessary for salvation. To quote again from Clark Pinnock, "The Bible does not teach that one must confess the name of Jesus to be saved." But this is exactly what the Bible *does* teach.

Two of Jesus' disciples, Peter and John, spoke about the necessity of confessing Christ when they were put on trial in Jerusalem. Concerning Jesus of Nazareth Peter said, "Salvation is found in no one else, for there is no other name under heaven given to men by which we must be saved" (Acts 4:12). It is worth emphasizing that Peter and John were addressing the leaders of Judaism when Peter said this. They did not suggest that Judaism was another way to God. Instead, they insisted on the necessity of coming to God in the name of Jesus Christ.

These disciples never abandoned their belief that salvation comes through Christ alone. John later wrote: "We have seen and testify that the Father has sent his Son to be the Savior of the world" (1 John 4:14). If his testimony had ended there, it would have been compatible with Christian pluralism. But

John continued: "If anyone acknowledges that Jesus is the Son of God, God lives in him and he in God" (v. 15). True, Jesus Christ is the Savior of the world. Yet, the only way to receive that salvation is by personally accepting him as Savior.

The apostle Paul taught the same thing. On one occasion a pagan asked him what he had to do to be saved. The man received a straightforward answer: "Believe in the Lord Jesus, and you will be saved" (Acts 16:31).

Furthermore, Paul insisted that genuine faith in Jesus Christ always produces verbal expression. No matter how explicit it is, a silent faith is insufficient for salvation.

> *If you confess with your mouth, "Jesus is Lord," and believe in your heart that God raised him from the dead, you will be saved. For it is with your heart that you believe and are justified, and it is with your mouth that you confess and are saved . . . for, "Everyone who calls on the name of the Lord will be saved." (Rom. 10:9-10, 13)*

It is difficult to imagine how the Bible could be any clearer on this point. A verbal testimony of explicit faith in Jesus Christ is essential for salvation.

The Only (Real) Problem

Assume for a moment that the Bible is right to say that Jesus is the only way to God. What was God thinking? Why did he make salvation so exclusive? Why did he decide that believing in Jesus is the only way to be saved?

1. *Sin is a universal problem.* The way to begin to answer such questions is to recognize that human beings have only one basic problem: sin. Sin is no longer a popular concept. It sounds old-fashioned and out-of-date. Moral failures now are treated as honest mistakes, bad habits, psychological disorders, or pathological diseases—anything but the sins they actually are.

A sin is anything that violates the moral law of the universe. Any time we do what God tells us not to do or fail to do what God commands us to do, we commit a sin. And every time we sin, we are found guilty in the sight of God and deserve divine judgment.

Christianity teaches that all the problems of the world spring from the human heart. All of humanity's economic, social, racial, military, and educational problems ultimately lie in the soul. They all come from the lust, hatred, greed, and rebellion of the human heart.

G. K. Chesterton, an English essayist, novelist, and biographer from the early part of the twentieth century, pointed out that original sin is the one doctrine that can be proven empirically from human history. Every generation confirms the wickedness of human beings. The history of humanity is a story of technological, medical, and artistic progress but also of moral failure. If anything, things are getting worse, for the twentieth century has been the bloodiest in history.

2. *Sin is your problem.* Since sin is the basic problem of humanity, it can be demonstrated from your own experience. Are there any sinners in your family? Many people experience great suffering because of the way they have been treated by their own family members.

What about your own sin? Have you ever taken a serious look at what is inside *your* heart? Here are a few questions to help: Do you ever exaggerate your abilities or virtues so other people will admire you? Is there anyone you secretly despise? Do you cut corners in your work?

You know that other people are like this too. And are you not just like them? Indeed, is it not true that your whole approach to life is essentially selfish, that you spend most of your time thinking about your own food, clothes, music, work, and entertainment?

The problem with humanity is sin. Anyone who takes a long, hard, honest look will discover that he or she is part of the problem. The Hebrew prophet Isaiah put it like this: "We all, like sheep, have gone astray, each of us has turned to his own way" (Isa. 53:6). His meaning is well-illustrated in the remote areas of Scotland where farmers do not bother to fence their land. The sheep roam wherever they please. It takes a team of sheep dogs to shepherd them back to the fold. Like so many sheep without a shepherd, human beings wander over the hills of immorality.

The mortal failure of the religions of the world—Christianity excepted—is that they do not take sin seriously enough. Other religions teach that people can become better on their own. Somehow, some way we can work our way back to God. We can keep the Torah, observe the eightfold path that leads to Nirvana, obey the Five Pillars of Islam, or become one with the universe. If there is a hell at all, we will get time off for good behavior.

Yet Christianity insists that everyone is a sinner through and through. Our minds, hearts, wills, and emotions are in rebellion against God. When it comes right down to it, the problem is not that there is only one way to God. The real problem is that human beings will not follow God at all. Paul, whom we have mentioned several times already, put it like this: "All have sinned and fall short of the glory of God" (Rom. 3:23). Like archers on the world's largest archery range, we all fall short of God's target. Far short. God's perfect moral target is miles away. We can see it, but we cannot hit it. Sadly, our moral shortcomings have brought great suffering into the world. They separate us from one another and from God, ultimately forever.

The fact of sin explains why the notion of a "virtuous pagan" or "anonymous Christian" is false. Christian pluralism assumes that there are people who would believe in Jesus Christ if they only had the chance. But this is not true. The sad truth is that everyone has the opportunity to worship the true God at this very moment but rejects it.

> . . . what may be known about God is plain to them, because God has made it plain to them. For since the creation of the world God's invisible qualities—his eternal power and divine nature—have been clearly seen, being understood from what has been made, so that men are without excuse. For although they knew God, they neither glorified him as God nor gave thanks to him, but their thinking became futile and their foolish hearts were darkened. . . . Furthermore, since they did not think it worthwhile to retain the knowledge of God, he gave them over to a depraved mind, to do what ought not to be done. (Rom. 1:19-21, 28)

This is the Bible's answer to the question, "What about those who have never heard?" Part of the answer, of course, is that God wants everyone to hear the good news about Jesus Christ. It is out of this concern that missionaries still take the Christian message to the remote parts of the world.

In the meantime, God's dealings with people who have never been introduced to Jesus are scrupulously fair. He has plainly revealed himself to everyone through his creation. And he only holds people responsible for what they know about him, not what they do not know. Yet even here they fail. They refuse to worship God for his power and eternity. Thus, as far as the Bible is concerned, there is no such thing as a righteous pagan. Like everyone else, those who have never heard about Jesus Christ are sinners in rebellion against God.

3. *Sin leads to judgment.* Worst of all, sin makes all of us guilty of eternal punishment. Our consciences remind us that there is a God who has the right to judge us for our sin. The Bible speaks of the wrath of God, which is God's holy hatred of sin in all its causes and effects. It is because of sin that "the wrath of God is being revealed from heaven against all the godlessness and wickedness of men who suppress the truth by their wickedness" (Rom. 1:18).

The wrath of God has already begun to be revealed. Sin always has its consequences. We see them in unfulfilled lives, broken relationships, and troubled national affairs. Disobeying God is ultimately self-destructive.

But the wrath of God has only begun, and one day it will be revealed in all its justice. There is a place of eternal separation from God, which the Bible calls hell. The Reformation theologian Martin Luther wrote, "All who are outside the Christian church, whether heathen, Turks, Jews, or false Christians and hypocrites, even though they believe in and worship only the one true God, nevertheless . . . remain in eternal wrath and damnation, for they do not have the Lord Christ" (*Larger Catechism*, II, 3).

The Bible describes the coming wrath plainly and personally:

> *Because of your stubbornness and your unrepentant heart, you are storing up wrath against yourself for the day of God's wrath, when his righteous judgment will be revealed. God "will give to each person according to what he has done." To those who by persistence in doing good seek glory, honor and immortality, he will give eternal life. But for those who are self-seeking and who reject the truth and follow evil, there will be wrath and anger. There will be trouble and distress for every human being who does evil. (Rom. 2:5-9)*

The Only Solution

Thank God there is a way to escape God's wrath. There is a solution to the problem of sin, a perfect payment for sin.

1. *The death of Jesus Christ.* The reason a payment for sin is necessary is because God is just. Sin has to be paid for. God is too holy simply to overlook it. Something needs to be done about our guilt, which is exactly what Jesus was doing on the cross.

The historical records show that Jesus of Nazareth was executed by Roman soldiers outside Jerusalem around A.D. 30. Of this there can be no reasonable doubt. There is also no doubt that Jesus was crucified, which was the common manner of execution for traitors and low-lifes in the Roman Empire.

But the Bible goes beyond these undeniable facts to their

interpretation. It teaches that when Jesus was crucified, he paid the penalty for sin. He offered a sacrifice—his life for the lives of his people. Because this sacrifice did away with sin, it is called the atonement. Because Jesus exchanged places with sinners, it is known as the substitutionary atonement.

The sacrifice Jesus offered was a perfect sacrifice because Jesus lived a sinless life. It was an infinitely perfect sacrifice because Jesus is God as well as man. This teaching—sometimes called "the doctrine of the incarnation"—is unique to Christianity. No other religion has ever claimed that its historical founder is the one and only supreme deity. Nor has any other religion ever dared to suggest that the one true God loves us enough to die for us. This is the glory and the beauty of Christianity. Because God is just, there had to be a payment for sin. Because God is love, he was willing to make the payment in the person of his own Son.

Earlier we quoted from the prophet Isaiah. Now we will quote him in full: "We all, like sheep, have gone astray, each of us has turned to his own way; but the LORD has laid on him the iniquity of us all" (Isa. 53:6). The sins of anyone who believes that Jesus died on the cross for him or her have been fully paid for.

By making this atonement for our sins, Jesus preserved the justice of God. Here we need to finish a quotation from Paul: "All have sinned and fall short of the glory of God, and are justified freely by his grace through the redemption that came by Christ Jesus" (Rom. 3:23-24). How else could God have preserved his justice and saved us from our sins at the same time? There is no other way, which is why there is no other Savior. God sent Jesus to die "to demonstrate his justice at the present time, so as to be just and the one who justifies those who have faith in Jesus" (v. 26).

The doctrine that salvation from sin comes through Christ alone (*solus Christus*) was one of the central doctrines of the Protestant Reformation in Europe. In his theological disputation at Zurich, the Swiss Reformer Ulrich Zwingli (1484-1531) explained it like this:

> The summary of the gospel is that our Lord Jesus Christ, the true Son of God, has revealed the will of his heavenly Father to us, and with his innocence has redeemed us from death, and has reconciled us with God. Therefore, Christ is the only way to salvation for all those who have been, are, and will be.

2. *The resurrection of Jesus Christ.* How can we be sure that we are reconciled to God? The proof that God the Father accepted Jesus' sacrifice as full payment for sin is that he raised Jesus from the dead. By itself the crucifixion of Christ is not Christianity. Christianity depends also on the resurrection of Christ.

Every Sunday Christians celebrate the fact that three days after Jesus died and was buried, he was brought back to life. His resurrection was and is the proof that he really is the Son of God. When Jesus was raised from the dead, he conquered death once and for all.

The historical evidence for the resurrection of Jesus Christ is persuasive. According to the standards for documentary evidence, it would hold up in any legitimate court of law. The New Testament documents are ancient and reliable. Furthermore, they record multiple eyewitness accounts of the Resurrection. Dozens, even hundreds, of people saw Jesus after he rose from the dead (see 1 Cor. 15:4-8). They not only saw him—they spoke with him and touched him.

In this case the eyewitness accounts are especially compelling because the first of them comes from a woman, Mary Magdalene (John 20:10-18). If a first-century Jew wanted to perpetrate a hoax, the last thing he would do is depend on the testimony of a woman. Women had no legal standing in the time of Christ. They were not even allowed to testify in a court of law. But Mary's testimony is accepted in the Bible because she was in fact the first person to see Jesus after he rose from the dead.

3. *The followers of Jesus Christ.* One more thing confirms that Jesus has solved humanity's root problem. The followers of Jesus were willing to die for their belief that Jesus rose from the

dead. If the Resurrection was a hoax, they would have recanted when they were tortured and threatened with death. This they refused to do. They were so convinced that Jesus was and is the Son of God that they were willing to die for their faith.

A good example of the way the threat of death sometimes makes people change their minds comes from the biography of Sabbatai Sevi (1626-1676). Sevi was one of the religious superstars of the seventeenth century. He was a Jewish teacher who claimed to be the Messiah, and hundreds of thousands of Jews believed him. In fact, after Jesus Christ, Sabbatai Sevi was the second-most popular messianic figure in the history of Judaism. Religious communities all over Europe and the Middle East worshiped him as the savior of the Jews.

Imagine their dismay when Sevi was captured by the Turks in 1666. Then imagine their shock when Sevi converted to Islam. Under the threat of death, Sevi and his closest disciples renounced the God of Israel and became Muslims. The threat of death made them tell the truth. They admitted that Sevi was not the Messiah.

It was different for Jesus and his disciples. They confirmed the truth of their claims with their own lives. Like Sabbatai Sevi, Jesus Christ could have saved his neck by renouncing his claim to be the Messiah. His disciples could have done the same thing. But the disciples had such strong confidence in the truth

of the resurrection of Jesus Christ that they took their fa
them to the grave. In the face of persecution and even death,
they continued to testify that Jesus died for their sins and rose
again from the dead.

If those disciples were right, they bear witness to the most
important event in history. Jesus Christ, the Son of God, has
been raised from the dead. The deepest problem of humanity has been solved. Sin has been paid for, and death has been
overcome.

If you believe these truths, then the death and resurrection of Jesus Christ are the most important events in your own
personal history as well. If you believe in him, your sins are
forgiven, and you will live forever with God. Jesus Christ is the
only way because he has solved your only problem.

FOR FURTHER READING

Anderson, Sir Norman. *Christianity and World Religions: The Challenge of Pluralism*. Downers Grove, Ill.: InterVarsity, 1984.

Carson, Donald A. The *Gagging of God: Christianity Confronts Pluralism*. Grand Rapids, Mich.: Zondervan, 1996.

Guinness, Os, and John Seel, eds. *No God but God: Breaking with the Idols of Our Age*. Chicago: Moody, 1992.

Horton, Michael Scott. "How Wide Is God's Mercy?" *modern* REFORMATION. January/February 1993, pp. 8-13, 30-32.

Lutzer, Erwin W. *Christ Among Other Gods*. Chicago: Moody, 1994.

Sire, James W. *The Universe Next Door*. Second edition. Downers Grove, Ill.: InterVarsity, 1988.

ALLIANCE®

OF CONFESSING EVANGELICALS

The Alliance of Confessing Evangelicals is a coalition of Christian leaders from various denominations (Baptist, Presbyterian, Reformed, Congregational, Anglican, and Lutheran) committed to promoting a modern reformation of North America's church in doctrine, worship, and life, according to Scripture. We seek to call the twenty-first century church to a modern reformation through broadcasting, events, publishing, and distribution of reformed resources.

The work centers on broadcasting—*The Bible Study Hour* with James Boice, *Every Last Word* featuring Philip Ryken, *God's Living Word* with Bible teacher Richard Phillips, and *Dr. Barnhouse & the Bible* with Donald Barnhouse. These broadcasts air daily and weekly throughout North America as well as online and via satellite.

Our events include the Philadelphia Conference on Reformed Theology, the oldest, continuing, national, reformed conference in North America; many regional events including theology and exposition conferences and pastors' events, including Reformation Societies who continue to join the hearts and minds of church leaders in pursuit of reformation in the church.

reformation21 is our online magazine—a free "go-to" theological resource. We also publish *God's Word Today* online daily devotional; *MatthewHenry*.org, a source on biblical prayer; Alliance Books from a list of diverse authors; and more.

The Alliance further seeks to encourage reformation in the church by offering a wide variety of CD and MP3 resources featuring Alliance broadcast speakers and many other nationally recognized pastors and theologians.

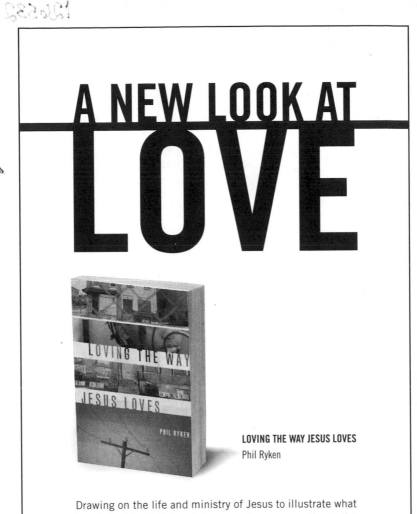

A NEW LOOK AT LOVE

LOVING THE WAY JESUS LOVES
Phil Ryken

Drawing on the life and ministry of Jesus to illustrate what love is and isn't, Ryken brings a unique perspective to the commonly quoted 1 Corinthians 13.